THE MAILBOX®

K.Tinkham

REAL-WORLD
Comprehension Practice

Skill-Building Activities to Help Students Read Real-Life Texts

- **Making Inferences**
- **Drawing Conclusions**
- **Determining Cause and Effect**
- **Comparing and Contrasting**

- **Identifying Main Idea**
- **Finding Supporting Details**
- **Determining Purpose**
- **Using Text Features**

Features real-life texts such as
- a newspaper article
- a drive-through restaurant menuboard
- classified ads
- movie listings
- an Internet search screen
- a sales flyer

and more!

Written by Stephanie Affinito and Stacie Stone Davis

Managing Editor: Hope Taylor Spencer

Editorial Team: Becky S. Andrews, Kimberley Bruck, Karen P. Shelton, Diane Badden, Thad H. McLaurin, Debra Liverman, Jennifer Bragg, Sherry McGregor, Karen A. Brudnak, Juli Blair, Hope Rodgers, Dorothy C. McKinney

Production Team: Lori Z. Henry, Pam Crane, Rebecca Saunders, Jennifer Tipton Cappoen, Chris Curry, Sarah Foreman, Theresa Lewis Goode, Greg D. Rieves, Barry Slate, Donna K. Teal, Zane Williard, Tazmen Carlisle, Marsha Heim, Lynette Dickerson, Mark Rainey

www.themailbox.com

©2006 The Mailbox®
All rights reserved.
ISBN10 #1-56234-697-0 • ISBN13 #978-156234-697-3

S0-AGO-231

Table of Contents

How to Use

This resource provides 24 real-world reading selections based on what kids encounter every day, such as movie listings, a sales flyer, or an Internet search screen. Each selection is accompanied by two follow-up practice pages for assessing students' comprehension of the selection. The reading selections can be used with individuals, small groups, or the whole class.

To use, simply make a copy of a real-world reading selection for each student or pair of students, or if desired, make a transparency of the page. Read aloud the selection or have your students read it independently. Then have students complete one or both of the follow-up practice pages.

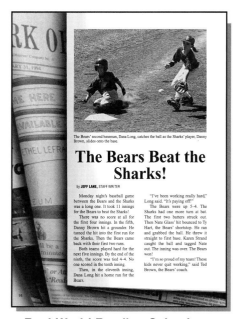

Real-World Reading Selection

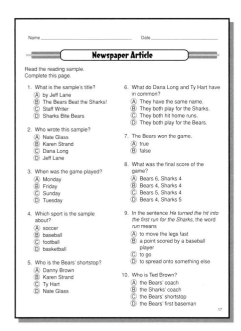

Practice Page 1
Assesses students' comprehension using a multiple-choice format

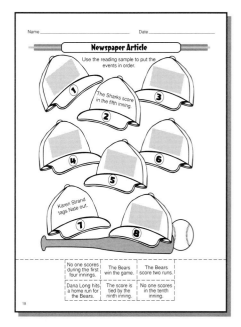

Practice Page 2
Assesses students' comprehension with an open format, such as short-answer questions, drawing a picture, describing a situation, labeling a diagram, or completing a graphic organizer

Supply List
Ms. Wells' Third-Grade Class
Rose Hill Elementary School

backpack
five #2 pencils
2 erasers
handheld pencil sharpener
3 wide-ruled spiral notebooks
3 two-pocket folders
glue stick
box of crayons (24 crayons)
pack of washable markers
box of facial tissues (for the class to share)
package of index cards

Please write your name on all of your supplies.

Name __Corinne__   Date _____

 **Supply List**

Read the reading sample.
Complete this page.

1. This supply list is for
   Ⓐ first grade
   Ⓑ second grade
   Ⓒ third grade
   Ⓓ fourth grade

2. How many crayons will each child need?
   Ⓐ 8
   Ⓑ 12
   Ⓒ 16
   Ⓓ 24

3. What kind of folders does each child need?
   Ⓐ folders with one pocket
   Ⓑ folders with two pockets
   Ⓒ plastic folders
   Ⓓ hole-punched folders

4. Each child needs
   Ⓐ wide-ruled spiral notebooks
   Ⓑ college-ruled spiral notebooks
   Ⓒ small notebooks
   Ⓓ large notebooks

5. Which supply will be shared with the class?
   Ⓐ markers
   Ⓑ pencils
   Ⓒ backpack
   Ⓓ tissues

6. What kind of markers are needed?
   Ⓐ permanent
   Ⓑ red
   Ⓒ washable
   Ⓓ thick

7. Which supply will hold the other supplies?
   Ⓐ lunch box
   Ⓑ folders
   Ⓒ backpack
   Ⓓ crayons

8. The teacher's name is
   Ⓐ Ms. Wells
   Ⓑ Mr. Wells
   Ⓒ Ms. Rose
   Ⓓ Ms. Stone

Name _____   Date _____

Supply List

Answer the questions.
Use the reading sample to help you.

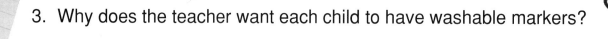

1. What should the child do to each of his or her supplies? _____

_____

Why do you think he or she should do this? _____

_____

2. Why do you think the teacher asks each child to have a backpack?

_____

_____

3. Why does the teacher want each child to have washable markers?

_____

_____

4. Why does the teacher want the children to share their boxes of tissues? _____

_____

_____

5. Why would the teacher want each student to have 24 crayons?

_____

_____

Attendance Policy

Students must be in school to learn. Children should attend school each day. A child may only miss school for the following reasons:

- The child is sick.
- There is a family emergency.
- The roads to school are not safe.
- There is a religious holiday.
- The child must go to a doctor.
- The child has an illness that can spread to others.

Send a note to school when your child returns. The note must tell why your child missed school. It also must have the date the child was absent. Be sure to sign the note and list your phone number.

Call the office if your child misses more than one day of school. The phone number is 555-0136. We may request a note from your child's doctor.

Children who get sick at school will be sent to the health aide. The aide will call you if your child needs to go home.

School Policies

Read the reading sample.
Complete this page.

1. There are _____ reasons why a child may miss school.
   Ⓐ three
   Ⓑ six
   Ⓒ seven
   Ⓓ two

2. A child may miss school to go to a doctor.
   Ⓐ true
   Ⓑ false

3. This sample is most likely written for
   Ⓐ teachers
   Ⓑ children
   Ⓒ parents
   Ⓓ the principal

4. When a child comes back to school, he or she must
   Ⓐ go to the doctor
   Ⓑ bring a note to school
   Ⓒ call the nurse
   Ⓓ call the teacher

5. Why should a student be in school each day?
   Ⓐ to learn
   Ⓑ to see the nurse
   Ⓒ to ride the bus
   Ⓓ to stay well

6. In the sample, to be *absent* means
   Ⓐ go to the doctor
   Ⓑ a report card
   Ⓒ to take a test
   Ⓓ to miss school

7. When the student comes back to school, he or she must bring
   Ⓐ a note from a doctor
   Ⓑ a note from the teacher to the parent
   Ⓒ a note that tells why he or she missed school
   Ⓓ a note for his or her friends

8. What happens if a child gets sick at school?
   Ⓐ The teacher goes to the health aide.
   Ⓑ The teacher calls the doctor.
   Ⓒ The child calls his or her parent.
   Ⓓ The child is sent to the health aide.

School Policies

If the note is complete, check the box.
If the note is not complete, write what is missing.
Use the reading sample to help you.

1.

Dear Ms. Davis,

Chad missed school on March 12. He was running a fever.

Mrs. Williams
555-0199

☐ _____

2.

Dear Ms. Davis,

Kelly stayed home Monday, May 1, because she had a headache.

Mr. Jones

☐ _____

3.

Dear Ms. Davis,

Sam broke his leg at soccer practice. That is why he missed school April 10 and 11.

Mr. Diaz
555-0121

☐ _____

4.

Dear Ms. Davis,

The snowstorm on the first of March caused our road to be blocked. So we had to stay home March 1 and 2.

Deb's mom
555-0133

☐ _____

5.

Dear Ms. Davis,

Josh still has the chicken pox.

Mr. Taylor
555-0154

☐ _____

6.

Dear Ms. Davis,

Tina has been very sick. She had to stay in bed May 2, 3, 4, and 5.

Mrs. Powers
555-0172

☐ _____

OSKP

THE ONE-STOP KIDS' PLACE

WE HAVE EVERYTHING KIDS NEED UNDER ONE ROOF!

Back-to-School Jacket Sale

August 24–September 1

Buy 1, Get 1 Free!
Jean Jackets for Boys and Girls, $30.00
sizes small, medium, large, and extra large
The jackets come in blue, black, or white.*

Girls' Sports Jackets With Matching Visors
$15.00
sizes 7–16
The jackets come in orange or purple.

Boys' Sports Jackets With Matching Caps
$16.00
sizes 8–16
The jackets come in red or green.

Fleece-Lined Jackets for Girls and Boys, $25.00!
Marked down from $35.00
This is the warmest jacket you can buy!
sizes small and extra large only
These jackets come in white, blue, and pink.*
*Colors may not be the same at every store.

Product Ad

Read the reading sample.
Complete this page.

1. When does the sale begin?
   Ⓐ September 1
   Ⓑ August 20
   Ⓒ August 24
   Ⓓ when school starts

2. The jean jackets come in these colors.
   Ⓐ blue, black, white
   Ⓑ blue or black
   Ⓒ blue, red, white
   Ⓓ red, yellow, blue

3. Which jacket does the ad say is the warmest?
   Ⓐ the boys' sports jacket
   Ⓑ the girls' sports jacket
   Ⓒ the jean jacket
   Ⓓ the fleece-lined jacket

4. How many kinds of jackets are on sale?
   Ⓐ five
   Ⓑ two
   Ⓒ one
   Ⓓ four

5. The sale ends on September 24.
   Ⓐ true
   Ⓑ false

6. Which jacket comes with a matching cap?
   Ⓐ visor
   Ⓑ fleece-lined jacket
   Ⓒ boys' sports jacket
   Ⓓ jean jacket

7. What do the stars by some of the lists of jacket colors mean?
   Ⓐ They are just decorations.
   Ⓑ All stores may not have all of the jacket colors.
   Ⓒ The jackets are not really on sale.
   Ⓓ The sale ends September 1.

8. If you buy a jean jacket, you can get any other jacket free.
   Ⓐ true
   Ⓑ false

Name ______________________ Date ____________

Product Ad

Use the reading sample to complete the chart below.

Feature	Jean Jacket	Boys' Sports Jacket	Girls' Sports Jacket	Fleece-Lined Jacket
for boys (Circle one.)	yes no	yes no	yes no	yes no
for girls (Circle one.)	yes no	yes no	yes no	yes no
sizes				
colors				
extra feature				
price				

Which jacket would you choose? Why? ______________________

Classified Advertisements

Pets for Sale

Dogs/Puppies

Free to a good home
Bulldog, boy
2 years old
Great with kids!
555-0184

Beagle puppy
Boy
$75
Call 555-0195

★★★★★★★★★★★★

Husky puppies
2 boys, 1 girl
$300 each
Call 555-0132

★★★★★★★★★★★★

Cute **Poodle Puppies**
8 weeks old
Have had 1st shots
3 boys, 3 girls
$100 each
555-0110

Pets for Sale

Dogs/Puppies

Lab puppies for sale
Black and tan
1 boy, 3 girls
$550 each
Tim 555-0141

Cats/Kittens

6 Free Kittens!
Near Glens Falls
555-0196

Other

Lovable **rabbit** for sale
$15
Call Ken at 555-0185

★★★★FREE Pets★★★★

Free to a nice family
2 brown **hamsters**
Cage and food included
Call 555-0176
Ask for Jane.

Place an ad!
Call 555-0148

Name _____   Date _____

 **Classified Ads**

Read the reading sample.
Complete this page.

1. How many of the ads are for dogs?
   Ⓐ three
   Ⓑ two
   Ⓒ eight
   Ⓓ five

2. What is the bulldog great with?
   Ⓐ kids
   Ⓑ adults
   Ⓒ finding bones
   Ⓓ doing tricks

3. The beagle is a girl.
   Ⓐ true
   Ⓑ false

4. What colors are the Lab puppies?
   Ⓐ tan and gold
   Ⓑ black and tan
   Ⓒ all black
   Ⓓ yellow and tan

5. What comes with the two brown hamsters?
   Ⓐ a cage and toys
   Ⓑ food and toys
   Ⓒ a cage and food
   Ⓓ nothing

6. What do the poodle puppies already have?
   Ⓐ their first shots
   Ⓑ a bath
   Ⓒ new toys
   Ⓓ collars

7. How many husky puppies are for sale?
   Ⓐ one
   Ⓑ two
   Ⓒ three
   Ⓓ four

8. Who can you call if you want a rabbit?
   Ⓐ Ken
   Ⓑ Tim
   Ⓒ Jane
   Ⓓ Tom

Classified Ads

Answer each question.
Use the reading sample to help you.

1. Which pets are free?

   _____

   _____

2. Which pets are not free?

   _____

   _____

   _____

3. Who do you think might read these ads? Why?

   _____

   _____

   _____

4. Which pet would you choose? Why?

   _____

   _____

   _____

5. Which pet would you not choose? Why?

   _____

   _____

   _____

The Bears' second baseman, Dana Long, catches the ball as the Sharks' player, Danny Brown, slides onto the base.

The Bears Beat the Sharks!

by **JEFF LANE,** STAFF WRITER

Monday night's baseball game between the Bears and the Sharks was a long one. It took 11 innings for the Bears to beat the Sharks!

There was no score at all for the first four innings. In the fifth, Danny Brown hit a grounder. He turned the hit into the first run for the Sharks. Then the Bears came back with their first two runs.

Both teams played hard for the next five innings. By the end of the ninth, the score was tied 4–4. No one scored in the tenth inning.

Then, in the eleventh inning, Dana Long hit a home run for the Bears.

"I've been working really hard," Long said. "It's paying off!"

The Bears were up 5–4. The Sharks had one more turn at bat. The first two batters struck out. Then Nate Glass' hit bounced to Ty Hart, the Bears' shortstop. He ran and grabbed the ball. He threw it straight to first base. Karen Strand caught the ball and tagged Nate out. The inning was over. The Bears won!

"I'm so proud of my team! These kids never quit working," said Ted Brown, the Bears' coach.

Newspaper Article

Read the reading sample.
Complete this page.

1. What is the sample's title?
   - (A) by Jeff Lane
   - (B) The Bears Beat the Sharks!
   - (C) Staff Writer
   - (D) Sharks Bite Bears

2. Who wrote this sample?
   - (A) Nate Glass
   - (B) Karen Strand
   - (C) Dana Long
   - (D) Jeff Lane

3. When was the game played?
   - (A) Monday
   - (B) Friday
   - (C) Sunday
   - (D) Tuesday

4. Which sport is the sample about?
   - (A) soccer
   - (B) baseball
   - (C) football
   - (D) basketball

5. Who is the Bears' shortstop?
   - (A) Danny Brown
   - (B) Karen Strand
   - (C) Ty Hart
   - (D) Nate Glass

6. What do Dana Long and Ty Hart have in common?
   - (A) They have the same name.
   - (B) They both play for the Sharks.
   - (C) They both hit home runs.
   - (D) They both play for the Bears.

7. The Bears won the game.
   - (A) true
   - (B) false

8. What was the final score of the game?
   - (A) Bears 6, Sharks 4
   - (B) Bears 4, Sharks 4
   - (C) Bears 5, Sharks 4
   - (D) Bears 4, Sharks 5

9. In the sentence *He turned the hit into the first run for the Sharks,* the word *run* means
   - (A) to move the legs fast
   - (B) a point scored by a baseball player
   - (C) to go
   - (D) to spread onto something else

10. Who is Ted Brown?
    - (A) the Bears' coach
    - (B) the Sharks' coach
    - (C) the Bears' shortstop
    - (D) the Bears' first baseman

Newspaper Article

Use the reading sample to put the events in order.

1

The Sharks score in the fifth inning.

2

3

4

5

6

Karen Strand tags Nate out.

7

8

No one scores during the first four innings.	The Bears win the game.	The Bears score two runs.
Dana Long hits a home run for the Bears.	The score is tied by the ninth inning.	No one scores in the tenth inning.

BIRTHDAY PARTY CENTRAL

This is **the** place for all your party needs!

Paper Plates
$1⁰⁰ per pack
(regular price, $2.00)

6 plates in each pack
Plates come in 10 colors and patterns!

Paper Cups
$1⁰⁰ per pack
(regular price, $1.75)

6 cups in each pack
Colors and patterns match the plates and napkins!

Plastic forks and spoons
6 of each for **$1.00**
(regular price, $1.50)

Napkins
12 napkins for **$1.00**
(regular price, $1.25)

Colors and patterns match the plates and cups!

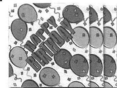

Wrapping Paper
2 rolls for **$1.00**

Pick from 25 colors and patterns!

Party Favors
Horns, tops, rings, toys, and more!

Mix and Match
12 for **$1.00**

Come see us at our new location!

Silver Springs Mall
1000 East Main Street
555-0172

Go to bpc@party.web for money-saving coupons!

Sales Flyer

Read the reading selection.
Complete this page.

1. How many paper plates come in a pack?
   - (A) ten
   - (B) six
   - (C) three
   - (D) five

2. When does the sale begin?
   - (A) March 23
   - (B) May 23–30
   - (C) May 30
   - (D) May 23

3. How many colors do the plates come in?
   - (A) ten
   - (B) six
   - (C) one
   - (D) two

4. In this flyer, the word *favors* means "small gifts."
   - (A) true
   - (B) false

5. What is the regular price for napkins?
   - (A) $1.00
   - (B) $1.50
   - (C) $1.25
   - (D) $ 2.00

6. The paper plates, cups, and napkins come in matching colors.
   - (A) fact
   - (B) opinion

7. When does the sale end?
   - (A) March 23
   - (B) May 23
   - (C) March 30
   - (D) May 30

8. How many colors do the cups come in?
   - (A) three
   - (B) six
   - (C) ten
   - (D) four

Sales Flyer

Read the reading sample.
Check each item that is on sale.
Use the reading sample to help you.

Birthday Shopping List

☐ birthday cake   ☐ horns

☐ candles   ☐ streamers

☐ plates   ☐ balloons

☐ forks   ☐ ribbons

☐ ice cream   ☐ bows

☐ spoons   ☐ birthday card

☐ punch   ☐ wrapping paper

☐ cups   ☐ gift bags

☐ a little toy for each
person

Movies

Good Old Days Drive-In

555-0154 • 1400 Main Street

Ruby the Rock Star (PG)
Love That Lion! (G)

Shows start at dusk. $10 per car.

Free popcorn!

DOWNTOWN THEATER

200 Center Street

All tickets are $7.00. Movies start at 12:00, 3:00, and 7:00.

Best Pals (G)

The Campout (G)

Space Surfers (PG)

Ruby the Rock Star (PG)

Good Morning, Mr. Mayor (PG)

Best Pals

Three friends enjoy the summer of their lives!

voices by
Jack Jackson
Tom Peck
Matt Peters

NOW PLAYING!

Lakeside Mall Cinema   Downtown Theater

Lakeside Mall Cinema

lakesidemall.web
All shows before 4:00 are $5.25. After 4:00, tickets are $7.50

Best Pals (G) 12:00 2:30
Good Morning, Mr. Mayor (PG) 4:45 7:00
Ruby the Rock Star (PG) 1:00 3:30 6:15
Kickball King (G) 12:25 3:00 5:50

CINEMA 3

58 River Road   **555-0162**

Good Morning, Mr. Mayor (PG)
4:15 6:05 8:20
The Campout (G)
2:00 4:25
Space Surfers (PG)
12:30 2:00 3:30

All shows before 5:30 are $6.00.
After 5:30, tickets are $9.00.

"A movie the whole family will love!"
—Doug Smith, *The Reviewer*

The Campout

"An action-packed adventure!"
—Carly Cooper, *Big City Times*

G

 **Movie Listings**

Read the reading sample.
Complete this page.

1. How many theaters are listed?
   (A) 2
   (B) 3
   (C) 4
   (D) 5

2. Which theater is on River Road?
   (A) Good Old Days Drive-In
   (B) Lakeside Mall Cinema
   (C) Cinema 3
   (D) Downtown Theater

3. What time can you see *Best Pals* at Lakeside Mall Cinema?
   (A) 12:00
   (B) 2:00
   (C) 11:30
   (D) 1:30

4. What does Good Old Days Drive-In give away?
   (A) movie tickets
   (B) popcorn
   (C) soda
   (D) prizes

5. *Good Morning, Mr. Mayor* is playing at both Lakeside Mall Cinema and Cinema 3.
   (A) true
   (B) false

6. When does *Best Pals* take place?
   (A) fall
   (B) winter
   (C) spring
   (D) summer

7. Which movie is not rated G?
   (A) *Best Pals*
   (B) *The Campout*
   (C) *Kickball King*
   (D) *Space Surfers*

8. How much would it cost to see *Kickball King* at 5:50?
   (A) $5.00
   (B) $7.00
   (C) $7.50
   (D) $9.00

9. What is the purpose of reading this sample?
   (A) to follow directions
   (B) to get information about movies
   (C) to read a made-up story
   (D) to form an opinion

10. Which showing of *Ruby the Rock Star* will cost the least?
    (A) 3:30 at Lakeside Mall Cinema
    (B) 6:15 at Lakeside Mall Cinema
    (C) 12:00 at Downtown Theater
    (D) 7:00 at Downtown Theater

Name _____ Date _____

Movie Listings

Write two details for each movie listing.
Use the reading sample to help you.
One has been done for you.

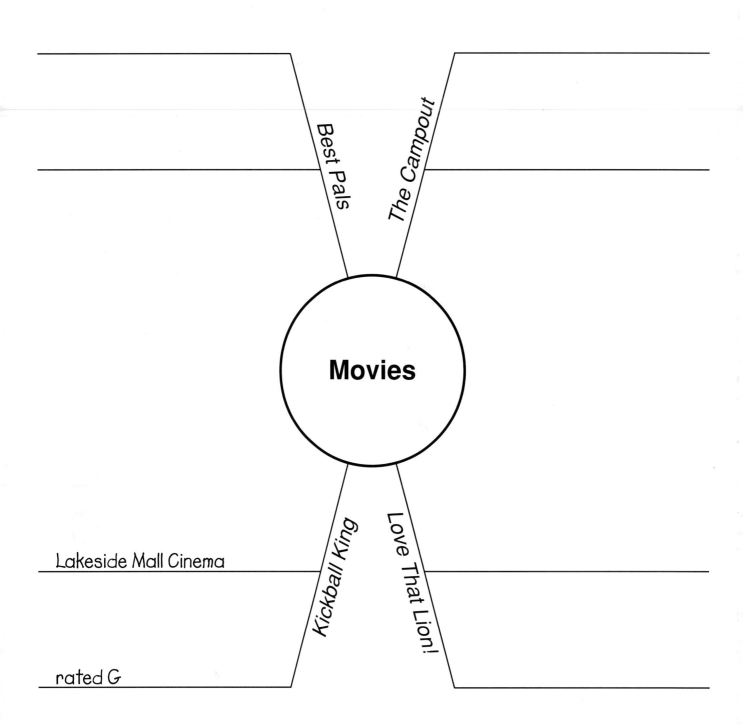

Best Pals

The Campout

Movies

Lakeside Mall Cinema

Kickball King

Love That Lion!

rated G

Poll Results: Find out on page 22 which state is our readers' favorite to visit.

Kids EXPLORE AMERICA

Celebrate the Fourth of July

Kids in Washington, DC, watch fireworks at the National Mall & Memorial Parks.

July
Kids Magazine Press
$3.50

Magazine Cover

Read the reading sample.
Complete this page.

1. What is the name of the magazine?
   - (A) *Kid Explorers*
   - (B) *Children Exploring the United States*
   - (C) *American Family*
   - (D) *Kids Explore America*

2. Which holiday is celebrated in this magazine?
   - (A) Labor Day
   - (B) Fourth of July
   - (C) Easter
   - (D) Halloween

3. This magazine costs $3.00.
   - (A) true
   - (B) false

4. Who is the quiz about?
   - (A) George Washington
   - (B) Abe Lincoln
   - (C) Uncle Sam
   - (D) Ben Franklin

5. Where would you look to enter the poetry contest?
   - (A) page 3
   - (C) page 15
   - (B) page 7
   - (D) page 22

6. What is the purpose of reading this sample?
   - (A) to learn what is in the magazine
   - (B) to follow directions
   - (C) to make an opinion
   - (D) to ask questions

7. Which of the these topics might be in the August issue?
   - (A) Halloween
   - (B) going back to school
   - (C) winter activities
   - (D) Thanksgiving

8. Which of these statements is a fact?
   - (A) The quiz on Uncle Sam will be easy.
   - (B) $3.50 is a lot of money to pay for a magazine.
   - (C) Kids watch fireworks in Washington, DC, on the Fourth of July.
   - (D) Poems are hard to write.

©The Mailbox® • *Real-World Comprehension Practice* • TEC60916 • Key p. 78

Magazine Cover

Complete the table of contents page.
Use the reading sample to help you.

July

Kids EXPLORE AMERICA

Page	Article
3	_____
____	Quiz: How much do you know about Uncle Sam?
8	Pretty Fun Parades
11	Favorite Foods for the Fourth
15	_____
____	Plan Your Own Bike Parade!
____	Poll Results: Our Readers' Favorite State to Visit

Kids Magazine Press

GO FISH!

for two to four players

1. Shuffle the cards. Deal six cards to each player. Spread the rest of the cards facedown on the playing surface to make a draw pile.

2. Look to see if there is a set of fish cards in your hand. (A set is four fish cards that are the same color.) If you have one, lay the set in front of you.

3. Choose one player to go first.

4. When it is your turn, ask another player for cards that will help you make a set. For example, if you have red fish cards, ask one player, "Do you have any red fish?" If the player has any, he gives all of them to you. Then you take another turn.

5. If the player does not have the card, he says, "Go fish!" Then you draw a card from the pile. If you draw the color you asked for, show it to the other players. Then take another turn. If you do not draw the color you asked for, put the card in your hand. Your turn is over.

6. Each time you make a set, lay it in front of you.

7. Continue playing until all ten sets are made. Count the sets in front of you.
   The winner is the player who has the most sets!

Look for other fun card games from Smith Sisters.

Game Rules

Read the reading sample.
Complete this page.

1. What is the object of the game?
   Ⓐ to get another player's cards
   Ⓑ to get pairs of cards
   Ⓒ to be the last player with cards
   Ⓓ to get the most sets of cards

2. In this game, what is a set of cards?
   Ⓐ the length of the game
   Ⓑ four cards that each have the same color fish on them
   Ⓒ something you do to the table
   Ⓓ playing four games in a row

3. At the beginning of the game, how many cards does each player get?
   Ⓐ two
   Ⓑ four
   Ⓒ six
   Ⓓ ten

4. This would be a good game for a two-year-old.
   Ⓐ true
   Ⓑ false

5. Why might a player tell you to "Go fish"?
   Ⓐ He does not have the color you asked for.
   Ⓑ He wants to help you get rid of your cards.
   Ⓒ He wants to help you get more cards.
   Ⓓ He is hungry.

6. ___ people can play this game.
   Ⓐ five to six
   Ⓑ zero to two
   Ⓒ eight to ten
   Ⓓ two to four

7. When is the game over?
   Ⓐ after 20 minutes
   Ⓑ when all of the sets are made
   Ⓒ when one player is out of cards
   Ⓓ after the oldest player has taken a turn

8. Go Fish! is a fun game.
   Ⓐ fact
   Ⓑ opinion

9. What do you do if you draw a card that is the color you asked for?
   Ⓐ show it to the other players
   Ⓑ put it in the box
   Ⓒ put it back in the pile
   Ⓓ put it in your hand

10. How many sets of cards are in the deck?
   Ⓐ eight
   Ⓑ nine
   Ⓒ ten
   Ⓓ eleven

Game Rules

Complete the flowchart.
Use the word bank to help you.

Word Bank	
color	sets
keep	again
draw	six
has	

How to play Go Fish!

Deal _____ cards to each player.

Lay down any _____.

On your turn, ask another player for a _____ that you need.

If the player _____ the card, go again!

If the player does not have the card, _____ from the pile.

If you pick the color you asked for, go _____.

If you do not pick the color, _____ the card. Your turn is over.

Macaroni and Cheese

You will need:

6 cups (c.) of water

3 tablespoons (tbsp.) of butter

3 tablespoons (tbsp.) of milk

To prepare:

1. Boil the water in a pot.

2. Stir in the macaroni. Boil for 11 to 13 minutes. Stir the macaroni often.

3. Drain the water from the pot without rinsing the macaroni. Pour the macaroni back in the pot.

4. Add the butter, milk, and cheese packet. Stir the macaroni and cheese until it is mixed.

5. Enjoy!

Want to add some fun? Add hot dog slices to your macaroni and cheese!

Name _____ Date _____

Read the reading sample.
Complete this page.

1. How long should you boil the macaroni?
   Ⓐ 14 to 16 minutes
   Ⓑ 11 to 13 minutes
   Ⓒ until the macaroni is cooked
   Ⓓ the directions don't say

2. How many steps are there?
   Ⓐ three
   Ⓑ four
   Ⓒ five
   Ⓓ six

3. What is the first step?
   Ⓐ Boil the water in a pot.
   Ⓑ Add the macaroni to the water.
   Ⓒ Add the milk and cheese.
   Ⓓ Stir the macaroni.

4. What is the abbreviation for tablespoon?
   Ⓐ tsp.
   Ⓑ TS
   Ⓒ tbsp.
   Ⓓ tbp.

5. Which of the following steps comes first?
   Ⓐ Stir in the macaroni.
   Ⓑ Drain the macaroni.
   Ⓒ Add the butter.
   Ⓓ Enjoy.

6. You should rinse the macaroni carefully.
   Ⓐ true
   Ⓑ false

7. Which ingredient does not belong in the macaroni and cheese?
   Ⓐ butter
   Ⓑ milk
   Ⓒ cheese
   Ⓓ cream

8. You need six cups of water for this recipe.
   Ⓐ fact
   Ⓑ opinion

9. How much milk do you need?
   Ⓐ 6 quarts
   Ⓑ 6 cups
   Ⓒ 3 tablespoons
   Ⓓ 3 cups

10. Which two ingredients do you need the same amount of?
    Ⓐ butter and milk
    Ⓑ milk and water
    Ⓒ cheese and water
    Ⓓ macaroni and butter

Name _____ Date _____

Number the steps to show the correct order.
Cut apart the boxes below.
Glue each box in front of its matching step.

  Stir the macaroni and cheese until it is mixed.

  Drain the water from the pot without rinsing the macaroni.

  Enjoy!

  Boil the water in a pot.

  Boil the macaroni for 11 to 13 minutes. Stir the macaroni often.

  Pour the drained macaroni back in the pot.

  Add the butter, milk, and cheese packet.

Stir in the macaroni.

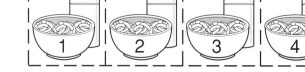

Pint-Size Pizzas

Ingredients:
4 English muffins
1½ c. pasta sauce
2 c. shredded mozzarella cheese

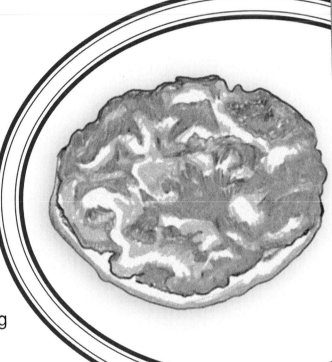

Directions:
1. Preheat the oven to 350°.
2. Cut the English muffins in half, and toast them in a toaster.
3. Spread about two table- spoons of sauce over each muffin. Then sprinkle the muffins with cheese.
4. Place the muffins on a baking sheet and place the sheet in the oven. Bake for ten min- utes or until cheese bubbles.
5. Let the muffins cool slightly before serving.

Makes eight small pizzas.

Note:
If you'd like to, add your favorite pizza toppings—such as mushrooms, peppers, or olives—before you bake the pizzas.

Easy-to-Make Recipes   65

Recipe

Read the reading sample.
Complete this page.

1. How many ingredients are needed to make the recipe?
   - Ⓐ 1½
   - Ⓑ 3
   - Ⓒ 4
   - Ⓓ 8

2. How hot does the oven need to be?
   - Ⓐ 100°
   - Ⓑ 200°
   - Ⓒ 250°
   - Ⓓ 350°

3. What should be done just before spreading on the pasta sauce?
   - Ⓐ Toast the English muffins.
   - Ⓑ Preheat the oven.
   - Ⓒ Sprinkle the English muffins with cheese.
   - Ⓓ Let the English muffins cool slightly.

4. This would be a good activity for a two-year-old.
   - Ⓐ true
   - Ⓑ false

5. Why do you think the recipe says to let the pizzas cool slightly before serving?
   - Ⓐ because pizza is a cold food
   - Ⓑ so they won't be too hot to eat
   - Ⓒ so you will have time to set the table
   - Ⓓ to give you time to rest

6. The pizzas should be placed on a baking sheet.
   - Ⓐ true
   - Ⓑ false

7. What does the "Note" section tell you?
   - Ⓐ that you can add other ingredients to the pizzas
   - Ⓑ the best brand of pasta sauce to use
   - Ⓒ foods you can serve with the pizzas
   - Ⓓ how to use a toaster

8. What is the purpose of the recipe?
   - Ⓐ to give an opinion
   - Ⓑ to tell a story
   - Ⓒ to tell how to make small pizzas
   - Ⓓ to ask questions

Recipe

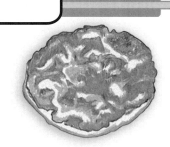

Answer the questions.
Write your answers in complete sentences.
Use the recipe sample to help you.

1. What do you need to make this recipe? _____

   _____

   _____

2. What does *preheat* mean? Why does the oven need to be preheated? _____

   _____

   _____

3. What should you do with the cheese? _____

   _____

   _____

4. Why do you think the recipe is called "Pint-Size Pizzas"? _____

   _____

   _____

5. If you made this recipe, would you add toppings to the pizzas or leave them

   plain? Why? _____

   _____

   _____

Welcome to Polly's Snack Shack

Burgers

Big and Heavy $1.85

Midsize Muncher $1.40

Little Load $0.99

Chicken

Crammer $2.10

Strips (6) $1.45

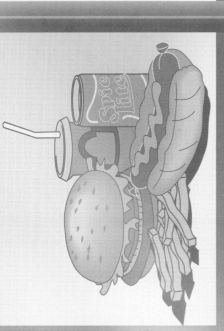

Sides

French Fries $1.00

Onion Rings $1.00

Salad $1.25

Fruit Cup $1.75

Special Deal

Big and Heavy Burger,
Fries, and a
Large Drink
Just $4.00!

Drinks

Lemonade, Soda, Tea

Small $0.50
Large $1.00

Milk Shakes $1.50
Any Flavor

Desserts

Ice-Cream Cone $0.95

Cookies $0.75

Cash Only

Drive-Through Menuboard

Read the reading sample.
Complete this page.

1. If you only have $1.00, which of these items could you buy?
   Ⓐ Big and Heavy Burger
   Ⓑ Little Load Burger
   Ⓒ Chicken Crammer
   Ⓓ Chicken Strips

2. How much does a large soda cost?
   Ⓐ $1.00
   Ⓑ $1.75
   Ⓒ $1.99
   Ⓓ $1.50

3. Where is this menuboard from?
   Ⓐ Chicken
   Ⓑ Burgers
   Ⓒ Polly's Snack Shack
   Ⓓ Special Deal

4. How many chicken strips are in an order?
   Ⓐ 2
   Ⓑ 4
   Ⓒ 6
   Ⓓ 8

5. A Chicken Crammer costs more than a fruit cup.
   Ⓐ true
   Ⓑ false

6. A small soda costs the same as a small tea.
   Ⓐ true
   Ⓑ false

7. What flavor of milk shake can you order?
   Ⓐ peach
   Ⓑ vanilla
   Ⓒ cookies and cream
   Ⓓ any flavor

8. Which statement is a fact?
   Ⓐ Six chicken strips are too many.
   Ⓑ The Big and Heavy Burger costs too much.
   Ⓒ A milk shake costs $1.50.
   Ⓓ A fruit cup tastes better than an ice-cream cone.

Name _____ Date _____

Drive-Through Menuboard

Write each menu item in the matching box.
Use the reading sample to help you.

Polly's Snack Shack

More than $1.00

_____ _____ _____

_____ _____ _____

_____ _____ _____

$1.00

_____ _____ _____

Less than $1.00

_____ _____

_____ _____

Come
again!

September
Elementary Lunch Menu

Mountain View
School District

Monday	Tuesday	Wednesday	Thursday	Friday	Offered each day:
				1 Hamburger French fries Tossed salad	• Peanut butter and jelly sandwich • Salad bar • Homemade soup
4 **Labor Day** No school!	**5** Cheesy nachos Green beans Applesauce	**6** Chicken patty Macaroni and cheese Fruit cup	**7** Hot dog Peas Fruit cup	**8** Pizza Carrot sticks Pineapple	**Prices** Lunch—$1.25 Milk—$0.30 Ice cream—$0.50
11 Fish sticks Corn Mixed fruit	**12** Hamburger Carrot sticks Apple slices	**13** Taco salad Rice Pears	**14** Sloppy joe Corn Apple crisp	**15** Ham and cheese wrap Tossed salad Peas	**September is Apple Month. Be healthy; have an apple!**
18 Shrimp poppers Peaches French fries	**19** Chicken strips Rice Green beans	**20** Grilled cheese Soup Grapes	**21** Pizza Corn Mixed fruit	**22** **Breakfast for lunch!** Egg sandwich or French toast sticks	
25 Baked chicken Mashed potatoes Pineapple	**26** Spaghetti Roll Mixed fruit	**27** Cheesy nachos Refried beans Tossed salad	**28** Hot dog French fries Carrot sticks	**29** **Teacher Workday** No school!	

Socce[r] Prac[tice] 4:30

Name _____   Date _____

Lunch Menu

Read the reading sample.
Complete this page.

1. This menu is for the month of
   - (A) August
   - (B) September
   - (C) October
   - (D) November

2. Why will lunch not be served on September 4?
   - (A) Nobody will be hungry.
   - (B) Lunches are not served on Mondays.
   - (C) It is a teacher workday.
   - (D) It is a holiday.

3. If you don't like the main dish on the menu, you can have
   - (A) cookies
   - (B) homemade soup
   - (C) apple slices
   - (D) a tuna sandwich

4. What is the main dish on September 13?
   - (A) Chicken patty
   - (B) Taco salad
   - (C) Grilled cheese
   - (D) Cheesy nachos

5. The price of a lunch is
   - (A) $0.30
   - (B) $0.50
   - (C) $1.25
   - (D) $1.50

6. When will pizza be served?
   - (A) September 1
   - (B) September 8
   - (C) September 21
   - (D) both September 8 and 21

7. What comes with the chicken strips on September 19?
   - (A) green beans
   - (B) peaches
   - (C) grapes
   - (D) apple slices

8. French toast sticks will be served on September 29.
   - (A) true
   - (B) false

Name _____ Date _____

Lunch Menu

Use the menu to choose four days to buy lunch.
Write each date on a line above a tray.
Illustrate the lunch on the matching tray.

_____   _____

   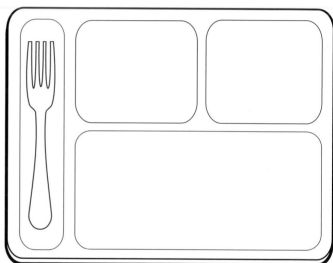

_____   _____

one dozen eggs
cooking oil
yellow cake mix
chocolate ice cream
three frozen pizzas
napkins
paper plates
icing
candles
birthday card
chocolate milk
two bags of chips

Grocery List

Read the reading sample.
Complete this page.

1. How many birthday cards are needed?
   - (A) 2
   - (B) 12
   - (C) 1
   - (D) 4

2. The items on the list will probably be used for
   - (A) Thanksgiving dinner
   - (B) a birthday party
   - (C) breakfast
   - (D) a picnic lunch

3. Which item will be found with the frozen foods?
   - (A) cake mix
   - (B) ice cream
   - (C) potato chips
   - (D) candles

4. Which item could be eaten right away?
   - (A) potato chips
   - (B) cake mix
   - (C) frozen pizza
   - (D) cooking oil

5. What kind of cake mix is needed?
   - (A) chocolate
   - (B) devil's food
   - (C) white
   - (D) yellow

6. To make this list easier to use, it could be set up
   - (A) in ABC order
   - (B) from biggest item to smallest
   - (C) in groups of items that can be found near each other in the store
   - (D) in complete sentences

7. White milk is needed.
   - (A) true
   - (B) false

8. Why is a grocery list helpful?
   - (A) It reminds you what to buy.
   - (B) It tells you where to find everything in the store.
   - (C) It tells you what is on sale.
   - (D) You learn how to spell words.

Name _____

Date _____

Grocery List

Sort the items from the grocery list.

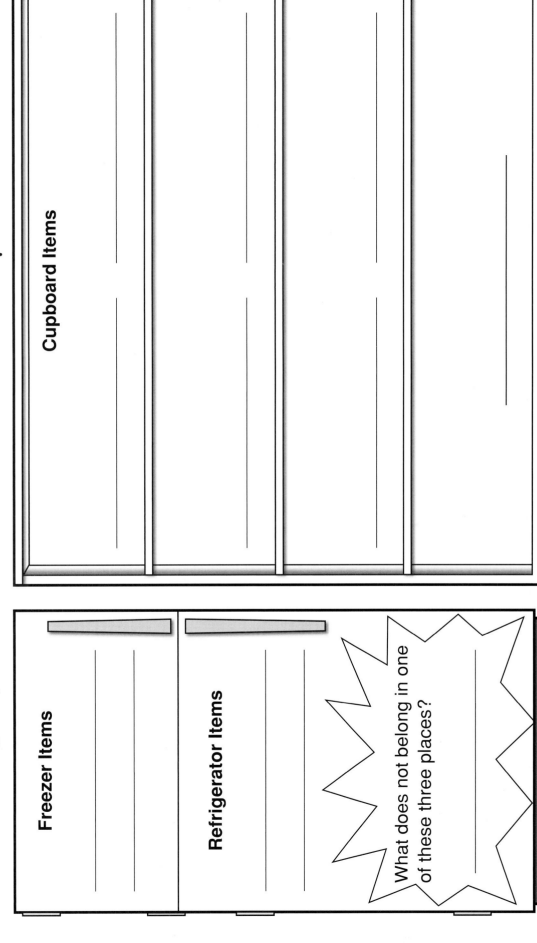

Cupboard Items

Freezer Items

Refrigerator Items

What does not belong in one of these three places?

Sign Up Now!

Camper's Name _____

Date of Birth _____

Parents' Names _____

_____

Address _____

_____

Home Phone _____

Work Phone _____

Email _____

Please return this form to

Camp Cody
123 Pinewood Way
Lake Lacy, Texas 00000

Daily Schedule

9:00	Camp begins/free play
9:30–10:30	Morning group games
10:45–11:45	Arts and crafts
12:00–12:30	Lunch
12:45–1:45	Afternoon group games
2:00–2:45	Pool time
2:45–3:00	Snack
3:00–3:30	Free choice
3:30	Camp ends

We also offer *Wow Weeks,* which focus on topics kids enjoy, such as

- gardening
- cooking
- music
- acting

It will be a summer of fun at

CAMP CODY!

June 1–August 28
For ages 6–10

Lake Lacy, Texas
www.campcody.web
123-555-0174

Kids at Camp Cody

go on nature walks, make arts and crafts, swim in the pool, play lots of games, and make lots of friends!

Each camper gets lunch and a snack each day.

JUST $150 A WEEK!

Summer Camp Brochure

Read the reading sample.
Complete this page.

1. You would see a five-year-old camper at Camp Cody.
   - (A) true
   - (B) false

2. What happens first in a camper's day?
   - (A) arts and crafts
   - (B) snack
   - (C) free play
   - (D) swimming

3. What clothes will a camper need between 2:00 and 2:45?
   - (A) a jacket
   - (B) a swimsuit
   - (C) shoes
   - (D) pants

4. What time does camp end?
   - (A) 2:45
   - (B) 3:00
   - (C) 3:30
   - (D) 5:00

5. Camp Cody is at Lake
   - (A) George
   - (B) Dale
   - (C) Lucy
   - (D) Lacy

6. Campers get to
   - (A) learn how to play soccer
   - (B) swim
   - (C) sleep over
   - (D) play computer games

7. To sign a child up for camp, parents need to list their
   - (A) home phone number
   - (B) birthday
   - (C) hair color
   - (D) favorite song

8. What happens after snack?
   - (A) pool time
   - (B) free choice
   - (C) lunch
   - (D) afternoon group games

Summer Camp Brochure

Camp Cody

Complete the chart.
Use the reading sample to help you.

9:00
Camp begins/
free play

9:30–10:30
_____
_____

Arts and crafts
_____

12:00–12:30
Lunch

Afternoon group games
_____

2:00–2:45
Pool time

2:45–3:00
_____

3:00–3:30
_____

3:30
Camp ends

©The Mailbox® • *Real-World Comprehension Practice* • TEC60916 • Key p. 79

48

http://gaga4games.web

GAGA4GAMES.WEB

Everything kids need to know about their favorite games!

Search for a game

| Learning | Car | Card | Playground | Video | Board |

Play Learning Games

Learn Car Games

Learn Card Games

Learn Playground Games

See Video Game Reviews

See Board Game Reviews

SEARCH BY GRADE

K

1

2

3

4

5

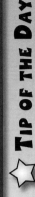

? POLL ?

How many other people do you usually like to play a game with?

0

1

2

3 or more

TIP OF THE DAY

Practice makes perfect. Keep trying!

You are visitor

0 5 2 3 8

Web Site Homepage

Read the reading sample.
Complete the page.

1. What is this Web site mostly about?
   - (A) playing fair
   - (B) rules
   - (C) games
   - (D) toys

2. How many people have visited this Web site?
   - (A) 52
   - (B) 5238
   - (C) 523
   - (D) 50238

3. Where do you click to learn how to play Go Fish?
   - (A) Play Learning Games
   - (B) Learn Car Games
   - (C) Learn Playground Games
   - (D) Learn Card Games

4. There are games just for sixth graders.
   - (A) true
   - (B) false

5. If you like to play games with four other people, which answer do you choose on the poll?
   - (A) 0
   - (B) 1
   - (C) 2
   - (D) 3 or more

6. This Web site shows reviews of video games and
   - (A) board games
   - (B) playground games
   - (C) first-grade games
   - (D) card games

7. If you cannot find what you need on this page, what should you do?
   - (A) ask your mom
   - (B) use the search box
   - (C) click on all of the sections
   - (D) give up

8. This Web site is made for
   - (A) teachers
   - (B) parents
   - (C) kids
   - (D) teenagers

Web Site Homepage

Complete the chart.
Use the reading sample to
help you.

Question	Yes/No
1. Can you learn card games at this Web site?	
2. Can you learn how to fly a kite at this Web site?	
3. Can you search games by grade at this Web site?	
4. Can you find the rules to computer games at this Web site?	
5. Does the Web site tell you how many people have used it?	
6. Does the Web site tell you where to buy games?	
7. Can you learn how to find library books at this Web site?	
8. Can you get help with writing reports at this Web site?	
9. Can you play games that teach you at this Web site?	
10. Can you find games to play at recess at this Web site?	

Hound Dog

skateboard parks

Search

Search results for *skateboard parks*

● Skateboard Parks
This site has a full list of the best skateboard parks in the world. It also has pictures of the different parks and maps to the parks.
www.skateboardparks.web

● Skate Parks USA
Use this site to find local parks as well as parks across the United States. Each park is rated by skaters.
www.skateparkusa.web

● North Woods Skate Park
Visit our indoor park in North Woods, Maine. We have 35,000 square feet of ramps and offer summer camps.
www.northwoodspark.web

● Circle City Skate Park
Learn about Circle City Skate Park in New York.
www.circlecityskates.web

● SOTEX Skate Parks
Learn about skate parks in southern Texas. This site has park facts, pictures, videos, and more!
www.sotexskates.web

Page 1 2 3 next

Internet Search Screen

Read the reading sample.
Complete this page.

1. What is the search topic?
   (A) parks
   (B) skateboard parks
   (C) skating
   (D) United States skate parks

2. What is the name of the search engine?
   (A) Hound Dog
   (B) Skateboard Parks
   (C) Search
   (D) Hot Dog

3. Which of these things can be found at the Skateboard Parks Web site?
   (A) videos
   (B) park ratings
   (C) maps
   (D) ramps

4. In what state is the Circle City Skate Park?
   (A) North Dakota
   (B) New Jersey
   (C) New Hampshire
   (D) New York

5. How many pages of results are there?
   (A) one
   (B) two
   (C) three
   (D) four

6. Which link tells about a park that will keep you dry while skateboarding?
   (A) Circle City Skate Park
   (B) North Woods Skate Park
   (C) Skate Parks USA
   (D) Skateboard Parks

7. What would you expect to find on page two of the search results?
   (A) more sites about skateboard parks
   (B) sites about where to buy roller skates
   (C) sites that tell how to ice-skate
   (D) sites about in-line skating

8. North Woods Skate Park has 3,500 square feet of ramps.
   (A) true
   (B) false

Internet Search Screen

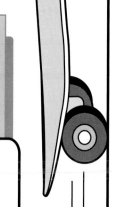

Write three details about each entry.
Use the reading sample to help you.
The first one has been done for you.

Topic: _____

Skateboard Parks	Skate Parks USA	North Woods Skate Park	SOTEX Skate Parks
list of the world's best skate parks			
pictures of the parks			
maps to the parks			

Evergreen City's
Five-Day Forecast

Sunday	Monday	Tuesday	Wednesday	Thursday
				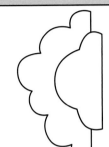
High: 37°F	High: 32°F	High: 43°F	High: 49°F	High: 51°F
Low: 29°F	Low: 27°F	Low: 32°F	Low: 39°F	Low: 35°F

Name _____   Date _____

Weather Chart

Read the reading sample.
Complete this page.

1. What city does this reading sample describe?
   (A) Green City
   (B) Pine Tree City
   (C) Green Tree City
   (D) Evergreen City

2. What is the title of the weather chart?
   (A) The Weather in Evergreen City
   (B) Evergreen City's Five-Day Forecast
   (C) Weather Forecast
   (D) Five-a-Day Forecast

3. There are two cloudy days on the chart.
   (A) true
   (B) false

4. Which day will have the highest temperature?
   (A) Sunday
   (B) Monday
   (C) Thursday
   (D) Friday

5. What season does this chart show?
   (A) winter
   (B) June
   (C) summer
   (D) January

6. The low temperature on Tuesday will be
   (A) 27°F
   (B) 32°F
   (C) 39°F
   (D) 43°F

7. On Sunday, you might want to wear
   (A) snow boots
   (B) shorts
   (C) sunglasses
   (D) flip-flops

8. What is the purpose of this chart?
   (A) to help you prepare for the weather
   (B) to decide which days to do your homework
   (C) to learn when the sun will set each day
   (D) to know who won the baseball game

Weather Chart

Answer the questions.
Write your answers in complete sentences.
Use the reading sample to help you.

1. Which day has the highest possible temperature? _____

   _____

2. Which days will be sunny? _____

   _____

3. What could you do outside on Monday? Why? _____

   _____

   _____

4. How are Wednesday's and Thursday's forecasts alike? How are they different?

   _____

   _____

   _____

5. Does Sunday's forecast seem better or worse than Thursday's forecast? Why
   do you think so? _____

   _____

   _____

Tip-Top Toys Store Directory

Action Figures

Models and Building Toys

Dolls

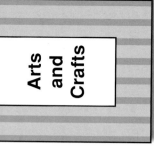

Arts and Crafts

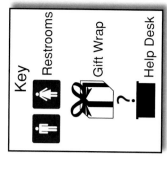

Key

Restrooms

Gift Wrap

Help Desk

Stuffed Animals

Games

Puzzles

?

Movies

Sports and Outdoor Items

Doors

Checkout Lanes

©The Mailbox® • *Real-World Comprehension Practice* • TEC60916

Name _____ Date _____

Read the reading sample.
Complete this page.

1. What is the name of the store?
   A Toy Store
   B Tip-Top Toys
   C Action Figures
   D Sports and Outdoor Gear

2. In which section will you find paints and markers?
   A Games
   B Models and Building Toys
   C Arts and Crafts
   D Puzzles

3. Where will you most likely find small cribs, clothes, and bottles?
   A Stuffed Animals
   B Dolls
   C Movies
   D Arts and Crafts

4. Which of these is next to the Sports and Outdoor Items section?
   A Action Figures
   B Games
   C Dolls
   D Stuffed Animals

5. Where is gift wrap found?
   A with the checkout lanes
   B next to Arts and Crafts
   C Models and Building Toys
   D in the Action Figures section

6. Where is the help desk found?
   A near the doors
   B next to the restrooms
   C behind the Dolls section
   D in the middle of the store

7. Why does a toy store have a help desk?
   A to help shoppers find toys they are looking for
   B to help shoppers pay for their toys
   C to help shoppers with their homework
   D to help shoppers fix their computers

8. Tip-Top Toys sells books.
   A true
   B false

9. How many pairs of restrooms are in the store?
   A zero
   B one
   C two
   D three

10. As you go from Puzzles to the checkout lanes, which section will you pass?
    A Dolls
    B Action Figures
    C Arts and Crafts
    D Movies

 # Toy Store Directory

Color each section of the toy store.
Use the map key to help you.

      Doors

---

Color Code

Action Figures = red	Movies = purple
Arts and Crafts = orange	Puzzles = brown
Dolls = yellow	Sports and Outdoor Items = black
Games = green	Stuffed Animals = white
Models and Building Toys = blue	

Math Center

Homework

Math: page 164, 1–12

Bring field trip permission slip.

Specials

Monday	Gym
Tuesday	Music
Wednesday	Art
Thursday	Gym
Friday	Music

Today is Tuesday.

8:30–8:50	Morning Work
8:50–9:50	Math
9:50–10:00	Snack
10:00–10:30	Library
10:30–11:00	Computer Lab
11:00–11:30	Writing/Journals
11:30–11:55	Lunch
11:55–12:15	Recess
12:15–1:15	Reading
1:15 –1:45	Special
1:45–2:30	Language Arts
2:30–3:00	Social Studies/Science
3:00–3:10	Cleanup
3:10	Dismissal

Daily Schedule

Read the reading sample.
Complete this page.

1. Reading the schedule will tell you what will happen in the classroom on Tuesday.
   - Ⓐ true
   - Ⓑ false

2. What will the class be doing at 11:00?
   - Ⓐ math
   - Ⓑ eating
   - Ⓒ writing/journals
   - Ⓓ singing

3. Which of these is in the afternoon?
   - Ⓐ library
   - Ⓑ reading
   - Ⓒ snack
   - Ⓓ morning work

4. What happens right after lunch?
   - Ⓐ recess
   - Ⓑ social studies/science
   - Ⓒ writing/journals
   - Ⓓ dismissal

5. What time is dismissal?
   - Ⓐ 3:00
   - Ⓑ 3:10
   - Ⓒ 3:15
   - Ⓓ 3:20

6. What time does lunch end?
   - Ⓐ 11:30
   - Ⓑ 11:45
   - Ⓒ 11:55
   - Ⓓ 12:15

7. Which special does the class have on Tuesday?
   - Ⓐ music
   - Ⓑ gym
   - Ⓒ art
   - Ⓓ lunch

8. If you are late and get to school at 10:00, which subject have you missed?
   - Ⓐ reading
   - Ⓑ language arts
   - Ⓒ writing
   - Ⓓ math

9. Computer lab is the best time of the day.
   - Ⓐ fact
   - Ⓑ opinion

10. Which of these begins at 1:45?
    - Ⓐ math
    - Ⓑ writing/journals
    - Ⓒ language arts
    - Ⓓ social studies/science

Daily Schedule

Draw pictures of two different things the class will do before lunch.

Draw pictures of two different things the class will do after lunch.

Table of Contents

Name _____ Date _____

Table of Contents

Read the reading sample.
Complete the page.

1. The table of contents is from a book about ___
   - Ⓐ the ocean
   - Ⓑ sharks
   - Ⓒ sea coral
   - Ⓓ life cycles

2. On which page would you find facts about shark senses?
   - Ⓐ page 25
   - Ⓑ page 31
   - Ⓒ page 36
   - Ⓓ page 39

3. In which chapter would you find out about different types of sharks?
   - Ⓐ Chapter 1
   - Ⓑ Chapter 2
   - Ⓒ Chapter 3
   - Ⓓ Chapter 4

4. Sharks are scary animals.
   - Ⓐ fact
   - Ⓑ opinion

5. Where could you find the definitions of unfamiliar words in this book?
   - Ⓐ the index
   - Ⓑ the glossary
   - Ⓒ the table of contents
   - Ⓓ the cover

6. The purpose of the table of contents is to help the reader find the information he or she is looking for.
   - Ⓐ true
   - Ⓑ false

7. In which chapter might you find out what sharks eat?
   - Ⓐ Chapter 3
   - Ⓑ Chapter 4
   - Ⓒ Chapter 5
   - Ⓓ Chapter 6

8. Which chapter will tell you how sharks can be helpful?
   - Ⓐ Chapter 3
   - Ⓑ Chapter 4
   - Ⓒ Chapter 5
   - Ⓓ Chapter 6

9. A table of contents can only be used in a nonfiction book.
   - Ⓐ true
   - Ⓑ false

10. Which information is not on the table of contents page?
    - Ⓐ the name of each chapter
    - Ⓑ page numbers
    - Ⓒ the author's name
    - Ⓓ chapter numbers

Table of Contents

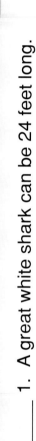

Write the best chapter number for each sentence.
Use the reading sample to help you.

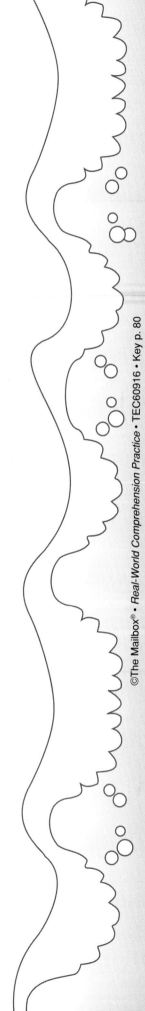

_____ 1. A great white shark can be 24 feet long.

_____ 2. Sharks can smell food even when it is far away.

_____ 3. When a shark is alive, its teeth are white.

_____ 4. Some sharks hatch from eggs.

_____ 5. Nurse sharks eat crabs, lobsters, and other sea creatures.

_____ 6. Sharks have been around for millions of years.

_____ 7. Most shark attacks happen in shallow water.

_____ 8. Some sharks have live babies.

GARDEN CENTERS

Alton Tree Nursery
212 State Street............................555-0182

Country Flower Farm
84 Reed Road 555-0143

Soil Sifters
230 East Road.............................555-0191

Stone Growers
31 Stone Road.............................555-0130

GIFT SHOPS

Becca's Christmas Store
32 Country Road 555-0147

Glen's Gift and Toy Shop
198 Abby Way 555-0185

Hill's Gifts and Flowers
780 Hill Avenue............................555-0100
(See our ad on this page.)

Hill's Gifts and Flowers

It's the cute little shop at the top of the hill!

We carry
- candles
- cards
- flower arrangements
- gift wrap

780 Hill Avenue • 555-0100

We are open Monday through Friday from
9:00 AM until 6:00 PM

Zane's Country Treasures
488 Creek Road 555-0111

GLASS REPAIR

Roy Hill's Glass
3418 Stewart Street......................555-0176

GROCERY STORES

Al's Corner Market
167 Oak Street 555-0139

Betty's Market
300 Main Street 555-0188

Big G Market
201 Maple Lane...........................555-0120

Clark's Superstore
76 Lake Road 555-0150
   Bakery 555-0151
   Deli 555-0152
   Photo Lab 555-0153
   Video 555-0154

HOBBY SHOPS

Hope's Craft Shop
102 Abby Way 555-0104

Luke's Train Shop
10 Main Street.............................555-0190

Tina's Model Planes
20 Topp Street 555-0171

Name _____ Date _____

 # Telephone Book

Read the reading sample.
Complete this page.

1. How many garden centers are listed?
   (A) two
   (B) three
   (C) one
   (D) four

2. You can order flowers from Hill's Gifts and Flowers on Sunday.
   (A) true
   (B) false

3. If you break a window, which store should you call?
   (A) Roy Hill's Glass
   (B) Al's Corner Market
   (C) Zane's Country Treasures
   (D) Betty's Market

4. Which item can you buy at Hill's Gifts and Flowers?
   (A) groceries
   (B) candles
   (C) windows
   (D) fabric

5. How is the phone book page like a dictionary page?
   (A) It has phone numbers.
   (B) It has guide words at the top of the page.
   (C) It has an ad on the page.
   (D) It tells what the words mean.

6. Which number would you call for the deli in Clark's Superstore?
   (A) 555-0104
   (B) 555-0171
   (C) 555-0153
   (D) 555-0152

7. How many types of stores are listed in the sample?
   (A) five
   (B) 11
   (C) four
   (D) ten

8. Clark's Superstore is the best grocery store.
   (A) fact
   (B) opinion

Telephone Book

Draw a line to match each item with the correct store.
Use the reading sample to help you.

1. a bakery on Lake Road   •   •   Alton Tree Nursery

2. yarn and knitting needles   •   •   Becca's Christmas Store

3. parts for a model train   •   •   Betty's Market

4. rocks for a yard   •   •   Clark's Superstore

5. a grocery store on Main Street   •   •   Hill's Gifts and Flowers

6. Christmas decorations   •   •   Luke's Train Shop

7. a new window   •   •   Roy Hill's Glass

8. a get-well card   •   •   Hope's Craft Shop

9. a gift shop on Creek Road   •   •   Stone Growers

10. a pine tree   •   •   Zane's Country Treasures

mit·ten *noun*
a covering for hands that has two parts:
one for the thumb and one for all of the
fingers *plural* **mittens**

mix *verb*
to blend things: *I mix the cake batter.*
mixed, mixing

mold

1. *noun* a fungus that can grow in
   wet places: *She found mold on the
   bread.*

2. *verb* to make
   something into a
   shape: *We
   molded clay
   into mammal
   shapes.* **molded,
   molding**

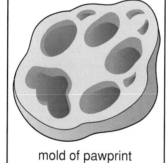
mold of pawprint

3. *noun* a container used to make a
   certain shape: *He made a mold of
   the fox's pawprint.*

mon·ey *noun*
the bills and coins that we use to buy
things

mon·key *noun*
a mammal with
hands and feet
that help it
climb and grab
things *plural*
monkeys

monkeys

mon·ster

1. *noun* something that is big
   and scary but is not real:
   *There are no monsters in the
   closet.* *plural* **monsters**

2. *adjective* very big, huge:
   *The truck's monster wheels
   made it tower above us.*

month *noun*
one of the 12 parts of a year

moon *noun*
a planet's satellite: *The moon
orbits Earth each month*

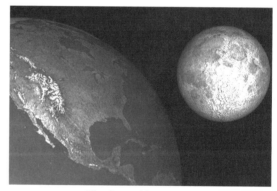
Earth and its moon

mos·qui·to *noun*
small flying insect that may spread
disease *plural* **mosquitoes**

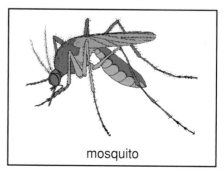
mosquito

Dictionary Page

Read the reading sample.
Complete the page.

1. Which word has three meanings?
   - (A) mitten
   - (B) monster
   - (C) mold
   - (D) moon

2. What are two kinds of money?
   - (A) paper and rubber
   - (B) bills and coins
   - (C) bills and paper
   - (D) rubber and coins

3. What has two parts and can keep your hands warm?
   - (A) a mitten
   - (B) a hat
   - (C) a scarf
   - (D) mold

4. Which is the meaning for the verb form of the word *mold?*
   - (A) a fungus that can grow in wet places
   - (B) a container used to make a certain shape
   - (C) to blend things together
   - (D) to make something into a shape

5. Why is there a dot in the word *mitten?*
   - (A) It looks nice.
   - (B) It shows the syllables.
   - (C) It shows the meaning.
   - (D) It shows that the word is a noun.

6. How many syllables does the word *mosquito* have?
   - (A) one
   - (B) two
   - (C) three
   - (D) four

7. Where would the word *mole* be listed on this page?
   - (A) after *mold*
   - (B) after *money*
   - (C) after *month*
   - (D) before *mix*

8. Which of these is not real?
   - (A) monkey
   - (B) mosquito
   - (C) monster
   - (D) moon

9. What is the purpose of the sample?
   - (A) to entertain
   - (B) to persuade
   - (C) to argue
   - (D) to inform

10. Which word is the plural form of *mosquito?*
    - (A) mosquitose
    - (B) mosquitoes
    - (C) mosquitois
    - (D) mosquito

Dictionary Page

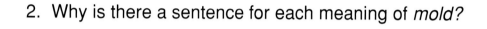

Use the sample to complete this page.

1. Would the word *mouth* go on this page? Tell why or why not.

_____

_____

_____

2. Why is there a sentence for each meaning of *mold?*

_____

_____

_____

3. Why are there pictures on the sample?

_____

_____

_____

4. Draw a picture for each of these words.

mitten	mix	month

Justin and Mo
GETTING READY FOR FIELD DAY

Hey, Mo! Will you come help me practice jumping over a hurdle? I want to win that race this year!

Sure! I'll be right there.

Justin, keep running. Keep running. Get ready. Now! Jump! Jump! Jump!

I did it!

Ah-ha!

I jumped! I did!

I know. You almost made it over! It was really close!

Comic Strip

Read the reading sample.
Complete the page.

1. What is Justin getting ready for?
   - (A) Field Day
   - (B) a school field trip
   - (C) going to bed
   - (D) dinner

2. What is the mouse's name?
   - (A) Justin
   - (B) Josh
   - (C) Mo
   - (D) giraffe

3. Justin is learning how to jump over hurdles.
   - (A) true
   - (B) false

4. What is Mo doing when Justin calls him?
   - (A) eating breakfast
   - (B) sleeping
   - (C) watching television
   - (D) reading a book

5. What is the purpose of the comic strip?
   - (A) to inform
   - (B) to entertain
   - (C) to describe
   - (D) to persuade

6. In the sample, Mo does not help Justin.
   - (A) true
   - (B) false

7. What happens when Justin tries to jump over the hurdle?
   - (A) He decides not to jump.
   - (B) He jumps over it.
   - (C) He trips and falls.
   - (D) He goes under it instead.

8. When Mo exclaims, "Ah-ha!" he means,
   - (A) "I have an idea!"
   - (B) "My shoe is untied."
   - (C) "Jump!"
   - (D) "Run!"

9. This comic strip was most likely written for
   - (A) nurses
   - (B) parents
   - (C) teachers
   - (D) school-age kids

10. What does Mo do to help Justin?
    - (A) He shows him how to jump.
    - (B) He chews the top of the hurdle to make it shorter.
    - (C) He promises Justin a prize.
    - (D) He jumps over the hurdle first.

Comic Strip

Use the sample to complete the page.

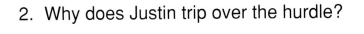

1. Is Mo at the track when Justin calls him? How do you know?

   _____

   _____

   _____

2. Why does Justin trip over the hurdle?

   _____

   _____

   _____

3. What does Mo do to help Justin jump over the hurdle?

   _____

   _____

   _____

4. Do you think Justin will win the race on Field Day? Tell why or why not.

   _____

   _____

   _____

Name ______________________

Page ______________________

1. (A) (B) (C) (D)

2. (A) (B) (C) (D)

3. (A) (B) (C) (D)

4. (A) (B) (C) (D)

5. (A) (B) (C) (D)

6. (A) (B) (C) (D)

7. (A) (B) (C) (D)

8. (A) (B) (C) (D)

9. (A) (B) (C) (D)

10. (A) (B) (C) (D)

Name ______________________

Page ______________________

1. (A) (B) (C) (D)

2. (A) (B) (C) (D)

3. (A) (B) (C) (D)

4. (A) (B) (C) (D)

5. (A) (B) (C) (D)

6. (A) (B) (C) (D)

7. (A) (B) (C) (D)

8. (A) (B) (C) (D)

9. (A) (B) (C) (D)

10. (A) (B) (C) (D)

©The Mailbox® • *Real-World Comprehension Practice* • TEC60916

 Note to the teacher: If desired, have students use the response sheet as a recording sheet for their answers for multiple-choice questions.

Answer Keys

Page 5
1. C
2. D
3. B
4. A
5. D
6. C
7. C
8. A

Page 6
Answers will vary. Possible answers include the following:
1. He should write his name on them. He'll know which supplies are his.
2. She wants him to have something to carry his supplies in.
3. Washable markers won't damage clothes.
4. There won't be enough room for each child to have a box of tissues on his desk.
5. Answers will vary.

Page 8
1. B
2. A
3. C
4. B
5. A
6. D
7. C
8. D

Page 9
1. complete
2. incomplete, no telephone number
3. complete
4. incomplete, no signature
5. incomplete, no date
6. complete

Page 11
1. C
2. A
3. D
4. D
5. B
6. C
7. B
8. B

Page 12

Feature	Jean Jacket	Boys' Sports Jacket	Girls' Sports Jacket	Fleece-Lined Jacket
for boys (Circle one.)	(yes) no	(yes) no	yes (no)	(yes) no
for girls (Circle one.)	(yes) no	yes (no)	(yes) no	(yes) no
sizes	small, medium, large, extra large	8–16	7–16	small, extra large
colors	blue, black, white	red, green	orange, purple	white, blue, pink
extra feature	buy 1, get 1 free	matching cap	matching visor	warmest
price	two jackets for $30.00	$16.00	$15.00	$25.00

Answers will vary.

Page 14
1. D
2. A
3. B
4. B
5. C
6. A
7. C
8. A

Page 15
1. the kittens, bulldog, and two brown hamsters
2. the beagle, husky puppies, rabbit, poodle puppies, and Lab puppies

3–5. Answers will vary.

Page 17
1. B
2. D
3. A
4. B
5. C
6. D
7. A
8. C
9. B
10. A

Page 18

Page 20
1. B
2. D
3. A
4. A
5. C
6. A
7. D
8. C

Page 21
The following items should be checked:
plates
forks
spoons
cups
a little toy for each person
horns
wrapping paper

77

Page 23

1. C	6. D
2. C	7. D
3. A	8. C
4. B	9. B
5. A	10. A

Page 24

Answers will vary. Possible answers include the following:

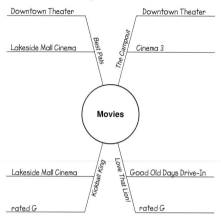

Page 26

1. D	5. C
2. B	6. A
3. B	7. B
4. C	8. C

Page 27

Page	Article
3	July 4th Across the United States
7	Quiz: How much do you know about Uncle Sam?
8	Pretty Fun Parades
11	Favorite Foods for the Fourth
15	Stars and Stripes Poetry Contest
16	Plan Your Own Bike Parade!
22	Poll Results: Our Readers' Favorite State to Visit

Page 29

1. D	6. D
2. B	7. B
3. C	8. B
4. B	9. A
5. A	10. C

Page 30

Deal ___six___ cards to each player.

Lay down any ___sets___.

On your turn, ask another player for a ___color___ that you need.

If the player ___has___ the card, go again!

If the player does not have the card, ___draw___ from the pile.

If you pick the color you asked for, go ___again___.

If you do not pick the color, ___keep___ the card. Your turn is over.

Page 32

1. B	6. B
2. C	7. D
3. A	8. A
4. C	9. C
5. A	10. A

Page 33

7 Stir the macaroni and cheese until it is mixed.

4 Drain the water from the pot without rinsing the macaroni.

8 Enjoy!

1 Boil the water in a pot.

3 Boil the macaroni for 11 to 13 minutes. Stir the macaroni often.

5 Pour the drained macaroni back in the pot.

6 Add the butter, milk, and cheese packet.

2 Stir in the macaroni.

Page 35

1. B	5. B
2. D	6. A
3. A	7. A
4. B	8. C

Page 36

Answers may vary.
1. You need English muffins, pasta sauce, and mozzarella cheese.
2. *Preheat* means *to heat before.* The oven needs to be preheated so it will be hot enough to bake the pizzas.
3. You should sprinkle it over the muffins.
4. It is called "Pint-Size Pizzas" because the pizzas are small and that is what pint-size means.
5. Possible answers: I would add sausage and pepperoni because that is how I like to eat pizza. I would leave the pizza plain because toppings can make the pizza too messy to eat.

Page 38

1. B	5. A
2. A	6. A
3. C	7. D
4. C	8. C

Page 39

More than $1.00		
Big and Heavy	Midsize Muncher	Crammer
strips	salad	fruit cup
milk shake	Special Deal	

$1.00		
french fries	onion rings	large drink

Less than $1.00		
Little Load	small drink	
ice-cream cone	cookies	

Come again!

Page 41
1. B
2. D
3. B
4. B
5. C
6. D
7. A
8. B

Page 42
Answers will vary. Each tray should show one lunch from the menu.

Page 44
1. C
2. B
3. B
4. A
5. D
6. C
7. B
8. A

Page 45

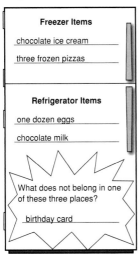
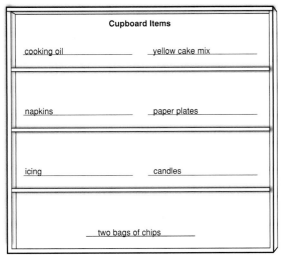

Freezer Items
chocolate ice cream
three frozen pizzas

Refrigerator Items
one dozen eggs
chocolate milk

What does not belong in one of these three places?
birthday card

Cupboard Items
cooking oil   yellow cake mix

napkins   paper plates

icing   candles

two bags of chips

Page 47
1. B
2. C
3. B
4. C
5. D
6. B
7. A
8. B

Page 48

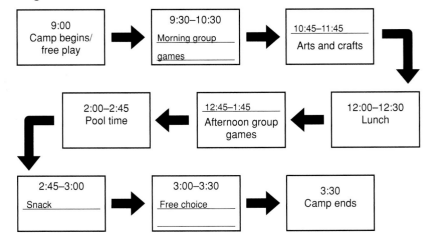

9:00 Camp begins/ free play → 9:30–10:30 Morning group games → 10:45–11:45 Arts and crafts → 12:00–12:30 Lunch → 12:45–1:45 Afternoon group games → 2:00–2:45 Pool time → 2:45–3:00 Snack → 3:00–3:30 Free choice → 3:30 Camp ends

Page 50
1. C
2. B
3. D
4. B
5. D
6. A
7. B
8. C

Page 51
1. yes
2. no
3. yes
4. no
5. yes
6. no
7. no
8. no
9. yes
10. yes

Page 53
1. B
2. A
3. C
4. D
5. C
6. B
7. A
8. B

Page 54
Answers may vary. Possible answers include the following:

Topic: Skateboard Parks
list of the world's best skate parks
pictures of the parks
maps to the parks

Skate Parks USA
local parks
parks across the United States
Each park is rated by skaters.

North Woods Skate Park
indoor park in North Woods, Maine
35,000 square feet of ramps
offers summer camps

SOTEX Skate Parks
information about skate parks in southern Texas
pictures
videos

Page 56
1. D
2. B
3. A
4. C
5. A
6. B
7. C
8. A

Page 57
1. Thursday will be the warmest.
2. Sunday and Tuesday will be sunny.
3. Answers will vary. Possible responses include the following: build a snowman, make a snow fort, make a snow angel, make snowballs. It should snow.
4. Wednesday and Thursday will both be cloudy days. They are different because Thursday's high temperature will be two degrees warmer than Wednesday's and its low will be four degrees colder.
5. Answers will vary.

Page 59
1. B
2. C
3. B
4. A
5. A
6. D
7. A
8. B
9. C
10. D

Page 60

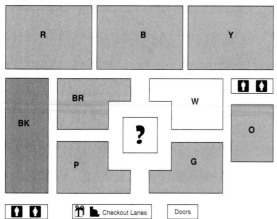

Page 62
1. A
2. C
3. B
4. A
5. B
6. C
7. A
8. D
9. B
10. C

Page 63
The top two boxes should show pictures of morning work, math, snack, library, computer lab, or writing.

The bottom two boxes should show pictures of recess, reading, music, language arts, social studies, science, cleanup, or dismissal.

Page 65
1. B
2. C
3. D
4. B
5. B
6. A
7. A
8. C
9. B
10. C

Page 66
1. 4
2. 8
3. 9
4. 2
5. 3
6. 1
7. 6
8. 2

Page 68
1. D
2. B
3. A
4. B
5. B
6. D
7. A
8. B

Page 69
1. Clark's Superstore
2. Hope's Craft Shop
3. Luke's Train Shop
4. Stone Growers
5. Betty's Market
6. Becca's Christmas Store
7. Roy Hill's Glass
8. Hill's Gifts and Flowers
9. Zane's Country Treasures
10. Alton Tree Nursery

Page 71
1. C
2. B
3. A
4. D
5. B
6. C
7. A
8. C
9. D
10. B

Page 72
Answers will vary.
1. no; The last word on the page is *mosquito. U* comes after *s,* so *mouth* would probably be on the next page.
2. The sentences are examples of how to use the word. They help explain the meanings.
3. The pictures help explain what the words mean.
4. Answers will vary.

Page 74
1. A
2. C
3. A
4. D
5. B
6. B
7. C
8. A
9. D
10. B

Page 75
Answers will vary.
1. Mo is not at the track. The cartoon shows him at home reading.
2. Justin does not jump high enough, and he falls.
3. Mo eats the top part of the hurdle so it will be lower.
4. Answers will vary.